MEXICO
Leading the Southern Hemisphere

MEXICAN
FACTS AND FIGURES

Mexico City is one of the largest cities in the world. More than 21 million people live in the city and its suburbs.

MEXICO
Leading the Southern Hemisphere

MEXICAN
FACTS AND FIGURES

MASON CREST
PHILADELPHIA

Mason Crest
450 Parkway Drive, Suite D
Broomall, PA 19008
www.masoncrest.com

©2015 by Mason Crest, an imprint of National Highlights, Inc.

Printed and bound in the United States of America.

CPSIA Compliance Information: Batch #M2014.
For further information, contact Mason Crest at 1-866-MCP-Book.

First printing
1 3 5 7 9 8 6 4 2

Library of Congress Cataloging-in-Publication Data
        on file at the Library of Congress

        ISBN: 978-1-4222-3229-3 (hc)
        ISBN: 978-1-4222-8694-4 (ebook)

Mexico: Leading the Southern Hemisphere series ISBN: 978-1-4222-3213-2

TABLE OF CONTENTS

MEXICO
Leading the Southern Hemisphere

KEY ICONS TO LOOK FOR:

 Text-dependent questions: These questions send the reader back to the text for more careful attention to the evidence presented there.

 Words to understand: These words with their easy-to-understand definitions will increase the reader's understanding of the text, while building vocabulary skills.

 Series glossary of key terms: This back-of-the book glossary contains terminology used throughout this series. Words found here increase the reader's ability to read and comprehend higher-level books and articles in this field.

 Research projects: Readers are pointed toward areas of further inquiry connected to each chapter. Suggestions are provided for projects that encourage deeper research and analysis.

 Sidebars: This boxed material within the main text allows readers to build knowledge, gain insights, explore possibilities, and broaden their perspectives by weaving together additional information to provide realistic and holistic perspectives.

TIMELINE

1000 B.C.	The Olmec civilization becomes a leader in development of writing, numbering, and astronomy.
400 B.C.	Olmec civilization disappears.
150 B.C.	Teotihuacán is built.
A.D. 750	Teotihuacán is abandoned.
300-900	Peak cultural growth of the Maya.
900-1200	Toltecs control much of Mexico.
1200	Aztecs begin to conquer other tribes for control of Mexico.
1325	Aztecs build Tenochtitlán.
1500	Aztecs control all land in central Mexico.
1517	Córdoba and Grijalva explore the coast of Mexico.
1521	Spanish take control of Mexico.
1810	Grito de Dolores calls for Mexico's independence from Spain.
1821	The Treaty of Córdoba grants Mexico its independence.
1810–1821	Mexican War of Independence is fought against Spain.
1862	France invades Mexico.
1867	Benito Juárez triumphs over the French, executes the Emperor Maximilian, and resumes his presidency.
1876	Porfirio Díaz begins his period of dictatorship.
1910	The Mexican Revolution begins.
1921	The end of the Revolution and the beginning of modern-day Mexico.

1938 President Cárdenas nationalizes the petroleum industry and takes control of Mexico's oil reserves.

1965 The Mexican government launches the Border Industrialization Program, which encourages the creation of small factories called maquiladoras.

1968 Mexico hosts the Summer Olympic Games, and violence breaks out during a student protest.

1994 The North American Free Trade Agreement (NAFTA) goes into effect in January.

2000 Vicente Fox, a PAN candidate, is elected president.

2006 The United States begins to construct a controversial fence along the border to reduce drug smuggling and illegal immigration. In December, Mexican president Felipe Calderón orders federal soldiers and police to intervene in turf wars among powerful drug cartels, beginning a period of violence known as the narco war.

2009 The Mexican government reports that more than 6,500 people were killed in drug-related incidents during the year, making it the deadliest year of the narco war.

2012 Enrique Peña Nieto is elected president of Mexico, receiving 38 percent of the vote. His election returns the PRI to power after 12 years of PAN rule. He is sworn in as president on December 1.

2014 Joaquin "El Chapo" Guzman, leader of the powerful Sinaloa drug cartel, is arrested by the Mexican military; in June and July, Mexico's national soccer team participates in the World Cup tournament in Brazil.

 ## Words to Understand

illiteracy—the inability to read or write.

immigrate—to move one's residence from one nation or area to another.

import—to bring a product into a country from another nation.

export—to ship a product out of a country to markets in other nations.

The Metropolitan Cathedral in Mexico City is the largest and oldest cathedral in North America. The oldest part of the church was built in 1573, when Mexico was a Spanish colony.

MEXICO TODAY

Today's Mexico is a mixture of many things. Ancient traditions contrast with modern technology; Amerindian traditions and languages mingle with Spanish customs; Catholicism blends with native religions; and poverty and wealth live side by side. Even the people of Mexico represent a blend of European and Amerindian ancestors.

Mexicans today are proud of their rich heritage and their beautiful land—but they also know that their nation has many problems. Wealth is not spread evenly among all members of the population; the rich are very rich, but the poor are very poor—and unfortunately, there are far more poor people in Mexico than there are rich people. Government corruption is a major problem, although there have been improvements in this area over the past decade. Corruption and economic instability have contributed to problems like shortages of health care, unemployment, *illiteracy*, and crime. And since the mid-2000s, Mexico has been torn apart by a nationwide conflict between various drug cartels—criminal organizations that are fighting for control of lucrative drug smuggling routes. Since 2006, the Mexican army and federal police have been waging the war against the drug cartels. More than 80,000 people have been killed in this vicious conflict, known as the narco war, yet the cartels continue to fight with each other, as well as with Mexican authorities.

As the southernmost nation in North America, Mexico is located between the United States to the north and the Latin American countries to the south. Mexico shares the language, heritage, and customs of much of Latin America—but it also has strong emotional and economic bonds with its northern neighbor. Living so close to the United States, Mexicans see the wealth and opportunities enjoyed by many Americans. They want these same benefits for themselves. As a result, millions of Mexicans have opted to leave their homeland and *immigrate* to the United States, hoping to find a better life there. Many Mexicans follow legal channels when they come to the U.S. looking for work; however, some sneak across the border illegally. If they are caught, they will be sent back to Mexico.

A homeless woman sleeps on a street in Mexico City. The gap between the wealthy and poor is a major problem in Mexico, as more than half of the population—over 60 million people—lives below the poverty line.

A Mexican soldier checks vehicles for drugs at a checkpoint on the U.S.-Mexico border in Ciudad Juárez. At the height of the narco war in 2008-09, this city on the Rio Grande had the highest murder rate in the world.

13

Due to their 2,000-mile-long shared border, Mexico's problems affect the United States. The U.S. government estimates that more than 70 percent of the illegal drugs—including marijuana, cocaine, and heroin—that are smuggled into the United States each year comes from drug cartels operating in Mexico. Since 2008, under a plan called the Mérida Initiative, the U.S. government has provided more than $1.2 billion in financial assistance to help the Mexican government wage the narco war. Mexico and the United States have also worked together to stop illegal immigration while enabling Mexican laborers to find jobs in the U.S., as well as on initiatives promoting clean air and water.

Many people believe that improving the economy of Mexico would reduce poverty, which in turn would alleviate problems like drug smuggling and immigration. Over the past 20 years, Mexico has been a leading proponent of free trade—allowing the exchange of goods between countries without imposing

14

Mexican defenders Héctor Moreno (left) and Miguel Layún (right) move to stop Brazilian star Neymar during a first-round game during the 2014 World Cup tournament in Brazil. Soccer (*fútbol*) is the most popular sport in Mexico, and the country has done well in international competitions, including a gold medal win in the 2012 Olympic Games.

taxes or other restrictions. The North American Free Trade Agreement (NAFTA) went into effect in 1994, and it has helped Mexico's economy to grow. This agreement between the United States, Canada, and Mexico removes trade restrictions between the participating countries. This means that the American and Canadian companies do not have to pay taxes when they buy or sell products in Mexico. It also allows them to operate their own manufacturing facilities, known as maquiladoras, in Mexico. Maquiladoras *import* the materials needed to manufacture a product, and then *export* the finished product to markets in the United States, Canada, and elsewhere. For example, fabric or sewing machines might be brought tax-free from the U.S. into Mexico, where those items are used to manufacture t-shirts in a *maquiladora*. The t-shirts could then be sold in the United States. Today there are more than 4,000 maquiladoras operating in Mexico, manufacturing electronics, clothing, automobiles, and many other consumer products.

The success of NAFTA encouraged the Mexican government to sign free-trade agreements with many other countries, including China, Japan, the European Union, and many countries of Central and South America. Today, Mexico has the world's 14th-largest economy, with a gross domestic product (the value of all goods and services produced in a year) valued at over $1.3 trillion in 2014.

Mexico is far more than its economy, its government, or its problems. Mexico is made up of people who are artistic, resourceful, and loving. Their strong sense of identity was forged in the fires of Mexico's long history, and that history now inspires the Mexican people to face the future with hope.

 ### TEXT-DEPENDENT QUESTIONS

What is the Mérida Initiative?

What is a maquiladora?

 ### RESEARCH PROJECT

Choose one of the Mexico's 31 states and find out more about its geography. What are the major mountains, rivers, deserts, or other natural features within the state? Print out a map of the state, and label important geographic features as well as major cities.

WORDS TO UNDERSTAND

immunity—a person's natural ability to resist diseases.

peso—Mexican unit of currency (money).

smallpox—a contagious disease that causes high fever and pus-filled
sores that leave deep scars.

The land known as Mexico has been home to many civilizations over the centuries. The Mayan city of Palenque, pictured at left, was inhabited from about 225 B.C. until A.D. 800.

THE HISTORY OF MEXICO

More than 3,000 years ago, the Olmec civilization flourished in the land that is now Mexico. These ancient people built cultural centers and left their artwork as reminders to today's world. They were followed by many other great cultures: the Teotihuacán civilization, the Mayans, and finally the Aztecs. By the early 16th century, the Aztecs ruled most of central Mexico.

When Hernán Cortés arrived in Mexico in 1519, looking to claim this land for Spain, many of the people ruled by the Aztecs were eager to join forces with him. They resented the Aztecs' rule, and they hoped that with the help of the Spanish they could be free at last. Meanwhile, the Aztec ruler, Montezuma II, mistook Cortés for one of the Aztecs' favorite gods, Quetzalcoatl. Montezuma opened his kingdom to the white strangers—and the Spanish repaid him by taking him hostage and eventually slaughtering many of his people.

In the 300 years that followed, Mexico's native peoples suffered under Spain's rule. Many of them died after being exposed to diseases like *smallpox*, for which they had no *immunities*. The Spanish put them to work on their haciendas, tried to take away their culture and religion, and refused to give them any voice in their government.

18

At last, in 1810, Father Miguel Hidalgo encouraged the native Mexicans to revolt against their Spanish rulers. Their initial battle failed, but the fight for independence could not be stopped. In 1821, Mexico at last won its freedom from Spain.

The years that followed, however, were full of turmoil for the nation. One leader after another took control of Mexico and then was overthrown. In the aftermath of the Mexican-American War (1846-48), Mexico lost most of its northern territory to the United States.

In 1861, Benito Juárez, of Amerindian descent, became president, and the country's fortunes took a turn for the better. Then, in 1863, the French invaded Mexico and made the Archduke Maximilian its emperor. Maximilian and his wife Carlota came to love the Mexican people, but they did not return his feelings. Four years later, Juárez drove the French out, executed Maximilian, and resumed his presidency.

After Juárez's death, Porfirio Díaz ruled the country from 1877 to 1911. Although Díaz worked to build his nation's economy, under his rule a small group of rich people benefitted while the poor became even poorer. In 1910, Francisco Madero called for a revolution against the Díaz dictatorship. Rebels like Pancho Villa and Emiliano Zapata joined forces with Madero, and together they brought an end to the era in Mexico's history known as the Porfiriato.

Benito Juárez (left) and Porfirio Diaz (right) were two of Mexico's most influential and important 19th century leaders.

The rebel leader Francisco "Pancho" Villa is fourth from left in this photo. Villa was one of the most famous leaders of the Mexican Revolution between 1910 and 1920.

The years that followed were still more troubled. Between 1913 and 1920, 10 different presidents ruled the nation, as revolutionary and government forces battled each other. Finally, in 1920, Álvaro Obregón became president. His government brought an end to the revolution and ushered in the modern era in Mexican history.

Álvaro Obregón

The years since then, however, have been far from peaceful. The Institutional Revolutionary Party (PRI) controlled politics, but under their leadership, the gap between the rich and the poor continued to widen. In 1968, before the Summer Olympics were scheduled to be held in Mexico City, the tension led to a student strike that quickly turned into a riot. Several students were killed, and international attention turned to Mexico's problems.

In 1970 the discovery of new oil reserves combined with the rising prices of oil to give Mexico's economy a much-needed boost. However, the nation's leaders again made foolish choices that plunged their country's economy into still

20

Vicente Fox served as president of Mexico from 2000 to 2006.

deeper hot water. As the ***peso*** was devalued in the early 1980s, the nation found itself in the midst of an ever-worsening economic crisis.

Mexico began to get back on track economically in the 1990s, thanks in part to passage of the North American Free Trade Agreement and other free-trade deals with foreign countries. Despite this, the country continues to deal with political instability and violence. In 1994, Ameridians in the state of Chiapas began a rebellion against the federal government, seeking greater rights.

Corruption, economic problems, and scandals eventually weakened the power of the ruling PRI. In 2000, the Mexican people elected Vicente Fox, the first non-PRI president in 70 years. During Fox's time in office, Mexico increased its international presence, especially in business and diplomacy. According to many statistics, Mexico's quality of life improved during the Fox administration.

Another fair, multi-party election took place in 2006. The winner was Felipe Calderón, who like Fox was candidate of the National Action Party (PAN). Calderón, who had been governor of the state of Michoacán, immediately

addressed the problem of drug-related crime. He sent 6,500 Mexican soldiers to Michoacán, ordering them to attack the operations of the drug cartel La Familia Michoacana. This initial operation soon expanded in scope, leading to a widespread conflict between Mexican federal authorities and the drug cartels. This narco war, as it is called, has led to the deaths of at least 80,000 people since 2006. Yet the drug cartels remain as powerful, and profitable, as ever, with annual revenue from drug smuggling estimated at more than $40 billion.

Felipe Calderón

21

In 2012, the PRI returned to power with the election of Enrique Peña Nieto as president. In the first years of his term, Peña Nieto's administration successfully passed new legislation intended to reform many aspects of Mexican government and life, including education, financial services, the energy sector, and telecommunications. His government also continued waging the narco war against the drug cartels.

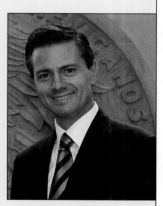

Enrique Peña Nieto

TEXT-DEPENDENT QUESTIONS

What Mexican of Amerindian descent became president in 1861?

Which party dominated Mexican politics from 1929 until the 2000 presidential election?

RESEARCH PROJECT

Using the Internet or your school library, do some research on a famous person from Mexican history, such as Hernán Cortés, Montezuma, Father Miguel Hidalgo, Benito Juárez, Porfirio Diaz, Francisco Madero, Emiliano Zapata, Pancho Villa, Venustiano Carranza, Álvaro Obregón, Vicente Fox, Felipe Calderón, or Enrique Peña Nieto. Write a two-page report about this person's life and accomplishments. Present it to the class.

 ## WORDS TO UNDERSTAND

catacombs—a network of underground passages or tunnels, sometimes used as a burial site.

infrastructure—a nation's system of public works, such as roads, railways, and schools.

lagoon—a body of water that is connected to a sea or bay.

murals—large pictures painted on walls.

rebozo—a long scarf worn by Mexican women.

serape—a colorful woolen shawl worn over the shoulders by Mexican men.

tropical—the region to the north and south of the equator, which is very hot and often has a high level of humidity.

Tourists enjoy the beach at Cancún, one of Mexico's most popular resorts. Each year, more than 20 million foreigners visit Mexico.

THE STATES OF MEXICO

Mexico's 31 states and capital city make up a land of rich diversity. The geography of this land is as varied as its people, for it contains deserts and *tropical* jungles, beaches and mountains, lava fields and deep-sea fishing resorts. The land is sprinkled with ancient archeological wonders, ethnic festivals, and world-famous art. No wonder Mexico is a favorite vacation spot for so many people.

BAJA CALIFORNIA NORTE

If you were to enter Mexico at its most western northern border, directly below San Diego, California, you would find yourself in the Mexican state of Baja California Norte. Tijuana is the border city that would give you your first glimpse of Mexican culture.

Tijuana, however, is like no other Mexican city. Although it is only the fourth largest Mexican city, it boasts the largest growth rate in the country. Mexicans from all over the country come to Tijuana, hoping to find a job in the many factories that send their wastes into the air and land around the city. Tijuana is dirty and not very pretty; there is not enough housing for the flocks of people that have come looking for work, and many make do with shacks built from

24

discarded packing crates, pieces of metal, and even cardboard boxes. Americans from across the border also crowd the streets of Tijuana, shopping for cheap Mexican crafts or looking for a good time in Tijuana's noisy nightlife. Others come to watch a jai alai game or a bullfight, and still others visit Tijuana for one of the international food festivals that are held each year in the city.

As you travel south from Tijuana, you will find yourself traveling down a long, narrow peninsula that reaches down between the Pacific Ocean and the Gulf of California. The land around you is dry and mountainous, and once you leave Tijuana's busy streets behind, the population is scarce, and the communities are small.

FACTS AND FIGURES ABOUT MEXICO

Total area: 755,866 sq. miles (1,958,201 sq. km)

Population: 120.2 million

Population growth rate: 1.21%

Urban population: 78.1%

Literacy rate: 93.5%

Gross Domestic Product (GDP): $1.845 trillion

GDP per capita: $15,600

Population below poverty line: 52.3%

BAJA CALIFORNIA SUR

A little less than halfway down the peninsula, you will find yourself crossing the state border into Baja California Sur. This state is much like its closest neighbor to the north, but it has even fewer people. There are, however, a few cities, and these are far different from sprawling, dirty Tijuana.

Guerrero Negro is the first city just across the border. The town was founded in 1937 when a North American company began extracting and exporting salt from the nearby *lagoon*. Even the air tastes salty in Guerrero Negro, and the salt plant there is the world's

The desert stretches across Baja California Sur, the least densely populated Mexican state.

largest. It produces over 6 million tons of salt a year. But one of the most fascinating events that takes place in Guerrero Negro has to do with whales rather than salt. Each year, between 10,000 and 20,000 gray whales come here, migrating as many as 6,000 miles from Alaska in the north. The whales come here to play and give birth to their young in Guerrero Negro's calm, warm lagoons.

Closer to the tip of Baja California's peninsula is the city of La Paz, the capital of Baja California Sur. Although the city's name means "the peace," the city has a long history of struggles. Its isolation made life hard for the settlers who tried to live there in the 1700s and 1800s. In the 18th century, disease wiped out much of the human population—and then in the 19th century other diseases attacked the oyster population in the neighboring bay, destroying the pearl industry that had once thrived there. Today, though, many tourists come to this city to enjoy the beautiful beaches and sport fishing. La Paz has found its peace at last.

26

SINALOA

From La Paz, you can take a ferry across the Gulf of California to the mainland. When you land, you will find yourself in Sinaloa, a long, narrow state that is sandwiched between the gulf and the foothills of the Sierra Madre Occidental. Like Baja California, Sinaloa has desert lands, but unlike the rocky peninsula, this state also has fertile valleys and mountainsides where thick vegetation thrives. The state has four main rivers—the Fuerte, the Sinaloa, the Mocorito, and the Piaxtla—and these supply the land with surface water. With the help of irrigation, the state produces farm products for Mexico, especially mangos, cotton, and sugarcane. It also has the largest canning factory in Latin America.

One of Sinaloa's main cities is Mazatlán. This is Mexico's chief Pacific port, and the country's largest shrimp fleet docks there. The residents of the city enjoy baseball and bullfights, while visitors love the beaches. For a sufficient tip from tourists, cliff divers will leap 40 to 50 feet into water below.

The harbor at Mazatlán, one of Mexico's most important Pacific ports.

The capital of Sinaloa is Culiacán, an agricultural center. It has been continuously inhabited longer than nearly any other city in in Mexico. Archeological evidence indicates that people have been living there since A.D. 900, although the modern city was founded by the Spanish in 1531. Despite its long history, however, the city attracts few tourists. Today it is modern and urban.

Sinaloa has been a center of the narco war, as the state is home to the powerful Sinaloa Cartel. This criminal organization is believed to make more than $20 billion a year from its drug trafficking operations. Although cartel leader Joaquin "El Chapo" Guzman was arrested by Mexican authorities in early 2014, most experts feel the Sinaloa Cartel will continue to dominate the illegal drug trade in Mexico.

SONORA

If you were to travel north along the Gulf of California from Sinaloa, you would find yourself entering the state of Sonora. In terms of land area, Sonora is the second-largest state in Mexico, and its population is growing as well. Like Baja California Norte, Sonora is located on the U.S.-Mexican border, which means that it is attractive to American industries looking to set up factories inside Mexico's borders. Big companies like Ford Motor Company, AT&T, Pepsico, Velcro USA, IBM, ITT Power Systems, and Sara Lee

Mexico's form of government is a presidential republic with a federal structure. The head of state is elected by a nationwide vote for a six-year term. Legislative power is exercised by a congress composed of the senate and the chamber of deputies. Estados Unidos Mexicanos (the United Mexican States) includes 31 states and the Federal District, which contains the capital, Mexico City.

27

28

manufacture from within Sonora. As a result of so much foreign investment, the state is Mexico's leading producer of electronic equipment, plastics, and chemical products.

Most of these factories are focused around Hermosilla, Sonora's capital. Although the city is not as close to the U.S. border as other communities, the city government has worked hard at attracting foreign companies. The city was first founded in 1700 as a military base for the Spaniards who were battling the Native Americans, and the old fort still stands at the heart of the city.

Around Hermosilla lies fertile farmland. Irrigation projects have brought water to the desert land, and wheat, corn, cotton, pecans, oranges, and grapes flourish under the warm sun. Although the Sonora Desert, the third largest desert in North America, stretches across much of the state, reclamation projects take advantage of the state's Yaqui, Sonora, and Mayo Rivers, opening up still more farmland for use.

CHIHUAHUA

Sonora's neighbor to the east is the state of Chihuahua, Mexico's largest state. To the north, Chihuahua is bordered by New Mexico and Texas. The Río Grande is Chihuahua's northeastern boundary line, separating it from the state of Texas.

Ciudad Juárez is the most important city on this boundary line. Like El Paso, its American sister city across the Río Grande, Juárez has grown in the valley carved out of the mountains by the great river. Like Tijuana and other border towns, Juárez sees a lot of American tourists coming across the border. Other sections of the city are packed with factories, most owned by American firms that have relocated in Mexico to take advantage of the low production

The official language of Mexico is Spanish, although many people speak the native Nahuatl and Maya languages.

A train runs through Copper Canyon, in the Sierra Madre mountain range of Chihuahua. Copper Canyon is four times as large as Arizona's Grand Canyon, and is almost 300 feet (about 90 meters) deeper than the Grand Canyon.

costs. The city was founded in 1581 by the Spanish, and the old sections of the city still exist.

If you cross the Chihuahuan Desert to the south of Juárez, eventually you will come to the state's capital, the city of Chihuahua. This city, founded in 1709, is the center for the state's mining operations and cattle raising. The lumber industry of the Sierra Madre mountains also contributes to much of the city's income. Although Chihuahua is exposed on the north to the desert's sandstorms, it also has rich pasturelands. During the Mexican Revolution, Pancho Villa had his headquarters here; his band of cowboys and bandits attacked the government of Porfirio Díaz from this base, and his home, Quinta Luz, is still one of the city's major attractions.

The state of Chihuahua contains people as diverse as the land itself. In the 1920s, Mennonites from the United States were attracted here by the rich pastures, and today they still maintain their communities in Chihuahua's agricultural areas. Like the Mennonites, the Tarahumara people live in isolation from the rest of the world, but their ancient native culture is far different. The Tarahumara sell their crafts in Chihuahua's cities, and then retreat to their simple lifestyle in Chihuahua's Sierra Madre mountains.

30

DURANGO

South of the state of Chihuahua lies Durango, a rocky, mountainous state whose capital is the city of Durango. If you are a moviegoer, this city may look familiar to you: more than 100 American, British, and Mexican films have been shot in the surrounding area. Many of the sets are still standing where John Wayne once hunted bandits in the desolate hills outside the city.

Although Durango makes money from the many movie sets that are scattered across this area, even more important are its rich natural resources. When the Spanish arrived in 1563, they discovered that gold, silver, lead, copper, and iron were hidden inside Durango's hills. One of the largest iron deposits in the world is just north of the city of Durango.

The wealth from these many mines can be seen in the city's huge cathedral and government buildings. The *Palacio de Gobierno* houses two of Mexico's great 20th-century **murals**, one by Francisco Montoya and the other by Ernesto Flores Esquivel.

Every July, the city of Durango celebrates for two weeks of *Feria Nacional*. The celebrations are wrapped around July 4, the day of the *Virgen del Refugio*, and July 22, the anniversary of Durango's birth in 1563. People come from all over the country to buy cows, bet on cockfights, and enjoy the good music and food.

ZACATECAS

As you continue your journey south, you will leave the state of Durango and enter Zacatecas, a state at the very center of Central Mexico's high desert. Although the land is dry, like Durango, it is rich with hidden minerals. Silver was once especially important to this area.

In the 1500s, a native Mexican gave a silver trinket to one of the early Spanish colonists, triggering a rush of hopeful miners to this area. The city of Zacatecas grew out of this boom. During the 300 years that Spain ruled Mexico, more than a billion dollars of silver and other precious metals were stripped from the mines of Zacatecas.

Benito Juárez and his government army defeated local rebels here in 1871. During the Mexican Revolution, Pancho Villa and his rebel forces won a victory over government forces in the hills of Zacatecas. Today, many of the silver mines have run dry, and the Revolution is long over, but the city of Zacatecas has kept its heritage of wealth and culture. Although not many tourists find their way to the center of Mexico, Zacatecas is well worth the trip. The streets are lined with colonial architecture, and the city continues to be a haven for artists and intellectuals.

AGUASCALIENTES

If you leave Zacatecas behind and travel south, you will cross the border into the state of Aguascalientes ("warm waters"). The state is named after its fresh hot springs, but the Spanish first called the region *"perforada"* or "perforated" because of the **catacombs** and tunnels that the native people had built beneath the land.

The capital of this small state is the city of Aguascalientes, a huge and growing industrial city. Neither the state or the city

MAJOR CITIES IN MEXICO AND THEIR POPULATIONS

Mexico City, 21.2 million
Guadalajara, 4.4 million
Monterrey, 4.1 million
Puebla de Zaragoza, 2.7 million
Tijuana, 1.75 million
León de los Aldamas, 1.6 million
Ciudad Juárez, 1.5 million
Querétaro, 1.1 million
San Luis Potosí, 1 million
Mérida, 1 million

has many attractions to bring tourists here, and as a result, travelers who do venture here often find that the people are unusually friendly and curious.

In April, however, people from around Mexico come to the city of Aguascalientes to celebrate the Feast of San Marcos. This month-long fiesta attracts artists, musicians, dancers, actors, and poets.

JALISCO

As you continue to travel south, you will enter the much larger state of Jalisco. Unlike the central states through which you've just traveled, Jalisco is bordered to the west by the Pacific Ocean. Lake Chapala, Mexico's second largest lake, also lies within its borders, and the Río Grande de Santiago flows out of the lake and across the state, providing the state with moisture.

The state's capital and largest city is Guadalajara. This city was first founded by one of the most brutal of the Spanish conquistadors, a man named Nuño de Guzmán. De Guzmán killed so many of the Amerindians in the area that very little of the native culture survived.

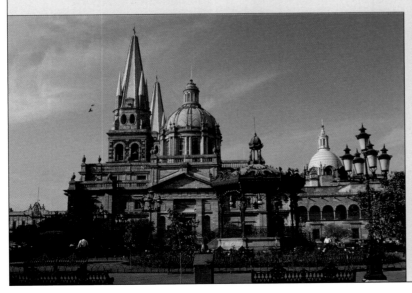

The cathedral of Guadalajara is one of the finest buildings in Mexico. Guadalajara is the capital of Jalisco, and the second-largest city in Mexico.

During the 19th century, when wealthy Mexicans wanted to escape the political unrest in Mexico City, they fled to Guadalajara, and here they surrounded themselves with a distinctive Spanish culture. The symbols of that culture—tequila, mariachi music, and the hat dance—have become important to the entire nation. Today, Guadalajara is Mexico's second-largest city. Although it has growing industries, it also still has its stately colonial architecture and fine museums.

Jalisco's many villages attract tourists with their colorful markets and quaint handicrafts. Tourists are also drawn to one of Jalisco's coastal cities, Puerto Vallarta. Visitors find here luxurious resorts and wide, clean beaches.

NAYARIT

If you make a quick trip north up Jalisco's Pacific coast, you will enter the small state of Nayarit, directly south of Sinaloa. Although Nayarit is small, it is one Mexico's leading tobacco growers. It also grows more varieties of fruit than any other state. The state's mountainous areas are scrubby and dry, but along the coast are fertile areas with abundant rain. The state also has two volcanoes: Ceboruco and Sanganguey.

Nayarit's capital city is Tepic. This city does not attract many tourists, but it is nevertheless known for its kindness to strangers. Many of the people who live here are very poor, and they often still wear the traditional clothing worn by their ancestors.

Although Tepic is a busy urban center, the mountains that surround it are nearly empty of people. The only residents of these high, wild areas are the Cora and Huichol Indians, who try to keep their ancient cultures intact. They venture into the towns and cities only to sell their artwork.

Tourists may not be attracted to the poverty and industrial parks of Tepic, but visitors do love Nayarit's beach towns. Nayarit's beaches lack the luxurious resorts found along other areas of Mexico's coast, but surfers, birdwatchers, and other adventuresome tourists enjoy the quieter atmosphere to be found in communities like San Blas.

COLIMA

If you leave Nayarit and once more cross Jalisco to the south, you will find yourself entering Colima. This is one of the smallest of Mexico's states, but this little area has a variety of geographical features. The beaches along the Pacific coast give way to farmland, while at the northeastern tip of the state, two volcanoes tower over the neighboring villages—and one of them is still active!

The capital city of Colima was founded in 1523 by the Spanish, and in the 1800s the city became an important stop when President Porfirio Díaz

A bird's-eye view of Manzanillo, the main port of Colima and one of the state's most important cities.

34

connected it by railway to the state's port city of Manzanillo. During the early 20th century, the turmoil caused by the Mexican Revolution wreaked havoc on the state of Colima, as battles raged back and forth across its fertile land. Slowly, though, the land recovered, and today its mining and shipping industries are prosperous. Tourists are also attracted to Colima's beaches and still-active volcano.

The state is a leading producer of lemons, as well as bananas, coconuts, corn, rice, and mangos. Factories are also moving into the state, producing beverages and clothing, and new discoveries of iron ore have made Colima one of Mexico's largest iron-producing states. The port of Manzanillo has become a hub for trade with the United States, Central and South America, and countries across the Pacific Ocean.

MICHOACÁN

Heading south along the Pacific Coast from Colima brings you to the state of Michoacán. When the Aztecs ruled Mexico, the Purépeche people lived around the shores of Lake Pátzcuaro, supporting themselves on the bountiful fish that lived in the lake. As a result, the Aztecs referred to these lands as "Michoacán"—which meant "country of fishermen."

The Purépeche people spoke a language that was different from any other spoken by the native people of Mexico, and they built terraced farm plots that were also unique in the land. Today archeologists believe these people probably migrated to Mexico from the South American country of Peru.

The Purépeche lived in what is now Michoacán from about 800 B.C. until the arrival of the Spanish in their lands in 1522. European germs did their part in decreasing the Purépeche population, but today the remnants of this culture still exist. Purépeche music, dances, and art are still common in Michoacán, and the language continues to be spoken in some of the smaller villages.

Morelia, the capital city of Michoacán, is full of both colonial elegance and markets designed to appeal to tourists. The surrounding land has become a productive agricultural area. The abundant rain, mild temperatures, and rich, red soil yield enormous corn harvests. Former Mexican president Felipe Calderón, who served from 2006 to 2012, was born in Morelia.

GUERRERO

As you continue your journey south along the Pacific Coast, you will enter the state of Guerrero, home to one of Mexico's most famous cities—Acapulco. Tourism is a thriving industry in this state, as visitors from all over the world flock here to enjoy the warm weather, elegant resorts, and beautiful beaches.

Other cities like Taxco and Ixtapa also attract their share of tourists, but the pace in these smaller cities is slower than in Acapulco, and the

The city can be seen behind the cliffs of Acapulco. This important city in Guerrero is a popular tourist destination.

atmosphere is gentler. Taxco is famous for its silver artisans, descendents of the original settlers who came to this city centuries ago seeking to make their fortunes in the silver mines.

Along Guerrero's coastline, the weather is often hot and steamy, but in the higher inland areas, the weather is better suited for farming. However, the tropical climate throughout much of the state means that the area's economy depends more on tourism than any other industry.

OAXACA

As you travel further along the Pacific coast you come next to the state of Oaxaca, a tropical land that suffers from economic poverty despite its cultural riches. Until recently, this state has been ignored by tourists, and its steamy weather made farming impossible. Now, the government is working to develop resort areas that will put Oaxaca on the map, and stimulate the faltering economy.

Historically, many different groups of people— the Zapotecs, the Mixtecs, the Aztecs, and Spaniards—have fought over this land. Over the past 2,000 years, more than 200 different tribes have inhabited this region. Today, over a million of the state's inhabitants still speak some form of

This ancient carving, which represents a dancer, was found at Monte Alban, Oaxaca.

38

native language, and a fifth of the state's population does not speak any Spanish at all. The native artisans are known worldwide for their hand-woven textiles, leather goods, and pottery.

Although tourism and the state's rich mines (especially coal and iron) offer hope for the future, many of the people of Oaxaca are disillusioned with their government. So many of them are desperately poor, and in the past the government has done little to help them. As they look at the rebels in the neighboring state of Chiapas, the people of Oaxaca consider joining the fight for better conditions.

CHIAPAS

Chiapas is at the tip of the Mexico Pacific coastline; if you were to continue your journey along the coast, next you would leave Mexico and enter the country of Guatemala. Until 1824, Chiapas was actually a part of Guatemala. Today, it is Mexico's poorest state.

Historically, Chiapas has always been a land of rebellion. In the 19th century, native people in the villages of Chiapas discovered *piedras hablantes*. These "talking stones" advised the people to rebel against the Spanish, and soon the Rebellion of 1869 was underway. However, the government quickly squashed the revolt.

In the 1930s, the Mexican government began the *ejido* system, where farmland was given to communities to own jointly. This helped the people of Chiapas, but their poverty continued. By the middle of the 1990s, many farmworkers in the state were earning as little as $1.75 a day.

In 1994, a group of Amerindians who called themselves Zapatistas began a revolt against the Mexican government. They occupied several towns in Chiapas,

There is beautiful scenery throughout mountainous Chiapas, including the steep walls of the Sumidero Canyon in Tuxtla Gutiérrez.

as well as Tuxtla Guitérrez, the state capital. The rebels' demands were for land, democratic reforms, health care, and education. The rebellion continued for more than a decade, although new legislation introduced by President Vicente Fox in 2003 resolved some of the rebels problems. Since then, the violence has diminished, although the Zapatistas continue to rule over some communities in rural areas of Chiapas.

CAMPECHE

If you are going to continue your travels in Mexico, now you must leave the Pacific coast and instead turn northeast to enter the state of Campeche. Campeche's coastline is to the northwest, on the Gulf of Mexico. The economy of Campeche depends on the oil industry, since the Bay of Campeche contains many of Mexico's offshore oil fields.

Oil is not the state's only industry, though. About 14 percent of the region's economy comes from wood and wood products, such as furniture.

An example of colonial architecture can be seen at the plaza in San Francisco de Campeche, where there is a cathedral as well as other buildings dating from the Spanish era.

The Maya once inhabited this land, and their ruins still dot the countryside. These ruins, however, tend to be smaller and more deeply hidden in the juggle than those found in Campeche's neighboring states; as a result, few tourists find their way to this state.

Quintana Roo

East of Campeche lies Mexico's youngest state, Quintana Roo. Many visitors insist that it is also Mexico's most beautiful region. A chain of coral reefs in the Caribbean Sea's turquoise waters guard the white beaches that stretch along the coastline. The land is filled with blue lagoons and underground caves.

Quintana Roo did not achieve statehood until the 1970s. Almost immediately, the Mexican government hit upon the idea of converting this tropical paradise into a tourist haven. They chose Cancún to be the center of their plan, and they worked hard to transform the city into a luxurious resort.

Tourists visit the Pyramid El Castillo, a Mayan ruin at Tulum, Quintana Roo. This state's economy is centered on tourism.

Their plan succeeded, and wealthy vacationers flock to Cancún every year. However, other tourists enjoy Quintana Roo's more traditional treasures—native artisans and a wealth of archeological sites. Another attraction created by the government is Sian Ka'an Biosphere Reserve, a 1.3-million-acre nature reserve that covers 10 percent of the state's land. The reserve offers lagoons, swamps, grasslands, forests, and 70 miles of coral reefs. It is home to hundreds of species of birds, fish, animals, and plants.

The Temple of Kukulcan is located at Chichén Itzá, Yucatán. Cities like Chichén Itzá and Uxmal were major centers of the ancient Mayan civilization.

YUCATÁN

The other state that shares the Yucatán Peninsula with Campeche and Quintana Roo is the state of Yucatán. For years, a lack of roads and communication systems kept this state from developing, but recently the government has worked to build the *infrastructure* of this area. As tourists are able to reach the state more easily, the economy is growing. Visitors come to see the impressive Mayan ruins at Chichén Itzá and Uxmal. Tourists also enjoy the Caribbean beaches and the native handicrafts for sale in open-air markets.

Yucatán grows citrus fruit, vegetables, sisal, and cantaloupes. Beekeepers have made the state one of the world's leading honey producers. Fishing, forestry, industry, and commerce are also beginning to grow in this state.

TABASCO

To continue along Mexico's Gulf coastline, you must first cut back through the state of Campeche, in order to reach the small state of Tabasco. The name comes from the Nahuatl word that means "waterlogged earth." The name is appropriate, since Tabasco has almost one-third of Mexico's water resources. The state's low plains are dotted with lakes and swamps, crossed by rivers, and covered with steamy jungles. The ancient Olmecs' enormous heads are scattered through the jungles, but the state has so few rocks that the Olmecs must have had to travel miles to get the huge pieces of stone they used to create their artwork.

Tabasco is one of Mexico's main oil-producing areas. In addition to oil, many maquiladoras have been constructed to produce products made from petrochemicals, such as plastics, soaps, fertilizer, and paint. The oil industry is bringing much-needed money to this state, but rickety shacks and shanties still cluster around the states' spreading refineries and factories.

The ornate façade of this church can be found in Cupilco, Tabasco. Most Mexicans are Christian, thanks to the influence of the Spanish in the 16th century. The majority of Mexicans (more than 82 percent of the population) are Roman Catholic, with various other Christian denominations making up another 10 percent).

43

44

VERACRUZ

As you journey west along the Gulf Coast, you will enter next the state of Veracruz, the first Mexican region to fall to Spanish rule when Cortés arrived on its shores. Today, the economy of this state, like Tabasco's, focuses on the oil industry. The state has more than one-fourth of Mexico's petroleum reserves; it supplies 17 percent of Mexico's energy; and it has the nation's second largest generator and only nuclear power plant.

The discovery of oil has caused a population explosion in Veracruz. At the beginning of the 20th century, only about one million people lived in this state; now about 7 million inhabitants make this the third most populated state in Mexico.

Veracruz's fishing fleet is also the largest in Mexico, and its oyster catch is among the biggest in the country. Agriculture and manufacturing are also

The castle of San Juan de Ulúa was built in 1528 to protect the harbor at Veracruz from Caribbean pirates. Veracruz was the first European settlement established on the American mainland; today, it is Mexico's most important seaport.

important parts of the state's economy, as is tourism. Visitors enjoy the many archeological sites. The southern part of the state, however, is largely undeveloped, and some tourists may find they like the slow, informal atmosphere in these small towns even better than they do some of the better known attractions. Local color is supplied by the *curanderos* (medicine men), who practice of mixture of conjuring and natural healing.

TAMAULIPAS

As you travel further along the Gulf of Mexico, you will enter the state of Tamaulipas. This states is bordered by Texas to the north, and many foreign industries are clustered along the border. American tourists enter the city of Matamoros from Brownsville, Texas. These tourists will shop for cheap Mexican trinkets and handicrafts in the many markets and stores.

Most of the residents along the border work in maquiladoras. Many inhabitants, however, have no work at all, and the area is full of desperate poverty. As a result, not many visitors enjoy visiting this area.

NUEVO LEÓN

Leaving the Gulf of Mexico behind and turning westward, you will enter the state of Nuevo León. The state has the third largest city in Mexico, and the largest city in northern Mexico—Monterrey.

Monterrey, the state's capital city, is a community of contrasts. Modern skyscrapers tower over colonial structures; wealthy businessmen live side by side with impoverished members of the lowest class. Wooden shacks offer photocopying services to the busy workforce, and beggars hold up their hands on the steps of new, shiny banks.

45

COAHUILA

Continuing west brings you to the state of Coahuila. The Río Grande forms the state's northern border, with Texas on the other side of the great river. Like other border states, foreign-owned *maquiladoras* have brought both problems and hope to the people of this state.

Venustiano Carranza

The capital city of Saltillo is proud that two national heroes were born there—Venustiano Carranza, a revolutionary general called the "father of the Mexican Constitution," and Francisco Madero, the man who put an end to Porfirio Díaz's power in 1911.

The first inhabitants of the region around Saltillo were Tlaxcalteca families, people who were weavers and craftsmakers by trade. The area is still famous for its colorful **serapes**. Every year, from July 18 to August 3, visitors from all over the country and the United States come to Saltillo for culture and artistry to be found at the *Feria de Saltillo*.

Francisco Madero

SAN LUIS POTOSÍ

If you leave Coahuila by its southeastern corner, you will find yourself in the central state of San Luis Potosí. In the 1500s, silver was discovered in the state's hills of San Pedro, and settlers came to the area hoping to make a fortune. However, the silver was soon depleted; today the mines still function but mainly as tourist attractions. In Real de Catorce, visitors can visit a ghost mining town.

Guanajuato City is an important cultural center.

However, the hills of San Luis Potosí proved to be full of other minerals as well. These mines and growing dairy farms form a large part of the state's economy. The village of Santa María del Río is the state's *rebozo* capital, and visitors come from all over to buy the fine silk shawls. The streets of San Luis Potosí, the state's capital with the same name as the state, are full of *vaqueros* and Burger Kings, primitive open-air markets and elegant, baroque architecture.

GUANAJUATO

Crossing San Luis Potosí's southwestern border will bring you next to the state of Guanajuato. This state is part of the great, bowl-shaped plateau known as El Bajío. The land here is fertile and rolling, and ever since the 16th century, the

48

area's silver mines have brought prosperity and shaped the course of its history. By the 1800s, the state supplied most of the silver that was minted into the country's coins. The capital city of Guanajuato became the commercial and banking center of this entire thriving region.

However, the city's wealth did little good for the ordinary people who lived there, and in the 19th century, Guanajuato was active in the Mexican fight for independence. Today, however, Guanajuato is a cultural center, sponsoring performances of drama, classical music, and ballet. Diego Rivera, the famous muralist, was born in Guanajuato, and his early works were deeply influenced by his birthplace.

QUERÉTARO

As you leave Guanajuato by crossing its eastern border, you will find yourself in Querétaro, another central state that nestles in El Bajío's fertile bowl. This small state was important in Mexican history, for here the country's current constitution was drafted. Here too the emperor Maximilian was put to death by

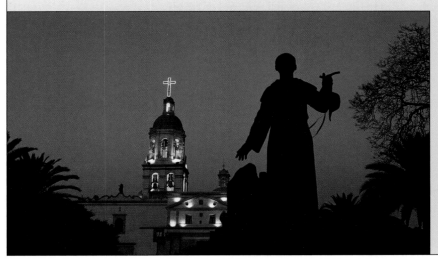

A statue of a Spanish missionary is silhouetted against the evening sky in Querétaro City. The blending of Spanish and native cultures produced the *mestizo* culture that is dominant in Mexico today.

Juárez's troops in 1867. His last words were, "Mexicans, I am going to die for a just cause: the liberty and independence of Mexico. May my blood be the last shed for the happiness of my new country!" Unfortunately, his blood was *not* the last shed for Mexico. Trouble and strife continued to haunt the nation, and the end of the Mexican-American War was finalized here as well. When Mexico signed the Treaty of Guadalupe Hidalgo in Querétaro, it gave away its northern territories to the United States. Nevertheless, today Querétaro is proud of its historic past, even as it struggles to deal with the modern problems of poverty and industrial pollution.

HIDALGO

Head southeast as you leave Guanajuato, and you will find yourself in the state of Hidalgo. Shadowed by tall volcanic mountains, this area was originally inhabited by the ancient Huastec people. When the Toltecs rose to prominence, they built their center in what is now the city of Tula. In the end, the Toltecs were swallowed by the Aztec empire— which ultimately gave way to the Spanish in the 16th century. Then in the War for Independence, the state again suffered from heavy fighting.

But despite the centuries of turmoil, the area is now an important cog in

Statues of Toltec warriors at the ancient city of Tula in Hidalgo.

Mexico's economic machine. Although it is often overlooked by tourists, food and precious metals flow out of the state. If you travel to Hidalgo, you can still see the ancient ruins of the Toltecs' city of Tula, outside the modern-day city. These ruins have temples, ball courts, palaces, and carved walls that depict serpents, jaguars, and eagles.

TLAXCALA

As you cross the southeastern border of Hidalgo, you enter the tiny state of Tlaxcala. The long-ago people who once lived here were the fierce enemies of the ancient Aztec city of Tenochtitlán. When Cortés arrived early in the 16th century, the Tlaxcalans were more than willing to join with his forces to fight the Aztecs they despised. King Charles V of Spain was so grateful for their help that he granted them titles of nobility.

Today, Tlaxcala is filled with reminders of both its Indian and colonial past. The town of Santa Ana Chiautempan has a 16th-century convent, while the ruins at Cacaxtla are considered to be one of Mexico's most impressive archeological sites. The massive ceremonial center was built and expanded between A.D. 600 and 750; it was abandoned in 1000. Visitors there can still see a huge, detailed mural that reveals much about the beliefs and lives of the people who once lived there.

PUEBLA

If you leave Tlaxcala going any direction except northwest, you will find yourself in the state of Puebla; Puebla nearly surrounds tiny Tlaxcala. Back in the early 1500s, Cortés's conquest of Mexico began to pick up steam when he reached this area. Many local tribes from the area became allies with the Spanish, hoping to free themselves from the Aztecs' hated rule.

A colonial-era church can be seen below the active volcano Popocatépetl, in Puebla.

Some of Mexico's oldest churches are in Puebla; they were built only months after Cortés's arrival. However, if you look inside some of these churches, you will see that the Spanish conquistadors and missionaries failed to fully Christianize the native people. Images from native mythology are mixed with Christian icons, revealing the mixture of these two religions that still exists in Mexico today.

Puebla's two volcanoes, Popocatépetl and Ixtaccíhuatl, are the second- and third-highest mountains in the country. According to native traditions, "Popo" was a warrior who loved Ixtaccíhuatl, an emperor's daughter. These star-crossed lovers remain loyal to each other, and "Popo" expresses his frustration and longing by smoking from time to time. Experienced climbers can go up to the top of both these mountains.

MORELOS

As you circle around to the northwest, you will cross the border into the state of Morelos. This small state first became a vacation spot when the Emperor

Maximilian built his summer home in Cuernavaca. Thousands of other Mexicans from Mexico City followed his example, taking advantage of Cuernavaca's "eternal spring," Tepoztlán's scenic beauties, and Cuautla's swimming areas.

Today's visitors also enjoy the many archeological sites to be found in Morelos. The ancient ceremonial center at Xochicalco contains Toltec pyramids and ball courts. Tepoztlán is famous for the towering cliffs that turned this village into a natural fortress. Outside the village, perched on one of the cliffs, is yet another ancient pyramid.

MÉXICO

As you continue your circle toward the northwest, you will enter the state of México. It may seem confusing to have a state with the same name as the nation, but Mexicans seem to enjoy using their names more than once. By now, you may have noticed that many of the states' capital cities have the same name as their state. The capital city of the state of México, however, is Toluca.

This state has green plains that rise up to snow-covered mountains. Its towns and cities are growing rapidly, as industries are drawn here to the heart of the nation. The city of Malinalco has a massive 16th-century church, as well the ruins of an Aztec temple.

MEXICO CITY, FEDERAL DISTRICT

At the very center of the circle you have been traveling is the nation's capital city, surrounded by the Federal District. It is the second largest population center in the world, with more than 21 million people living in 220 *colonias* (neighborhoods). One quarter of the country's entire population lives in the Federal District, and the area covers 522 square miles.

The city is the nation's cultural and economic center as well. Built on the foundations of the Aztec city of Tenochtitlán, the Federal District contains Aztec ruins, the enormous Metropolitan Cathedral, the Palace of Fine Arts, and many spectacular murals and mosaics by world-renowned artists like Rivera, Orozco, and Siqueiros.

Despite its beauty, the Federal District has its problems as well, just as the rest of Mexico does. Air pollution is a growing hazard over the city's ancient foundations and modern walls; overcrowding is a real problem as well, as more and more people come to the Federal District, seeking work in the growing industrial areas; and poverty is an ever-present tragedy here, as it is throughout the rest of the country.

But like the rest of Mexico, the Federal District is full of vitality and hope. Its people use the triumphs of the past as a foundation as they struggle to build a better future.

TEXT-DEPENDENT QUESTIONS

Where do the Tarahumara people live?

What Mexican presidents were born in the state of Coahuila?

Which Mexican states are known for production of oil?

RESEARCH PROJECT

Learn more about the Mexican Revolution, a period of turmoil from 1910 to 1921 during which approximately 900,000 Mexicans lost their lives. What were the causes of the Revolution? What major social and political reforms occurred in Mexico as a result of the Revolution? Did these changes affect the lives of most Mexicans, and if so, how?

54

APPENDIX: MAPS OF MEXICO

THE CENTRAL STATES OF MEXICO

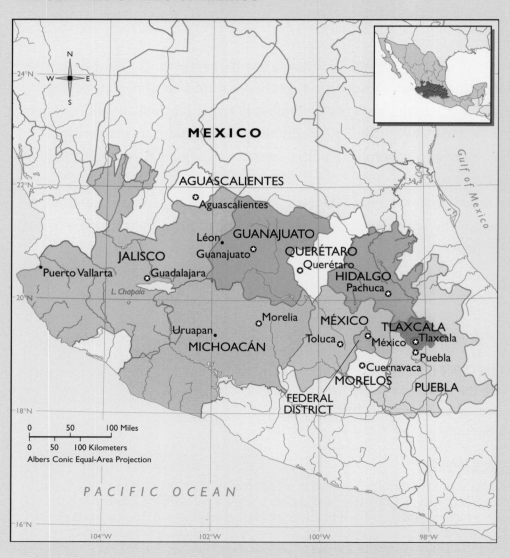

THE NORTHERN STATES OF MEXICO

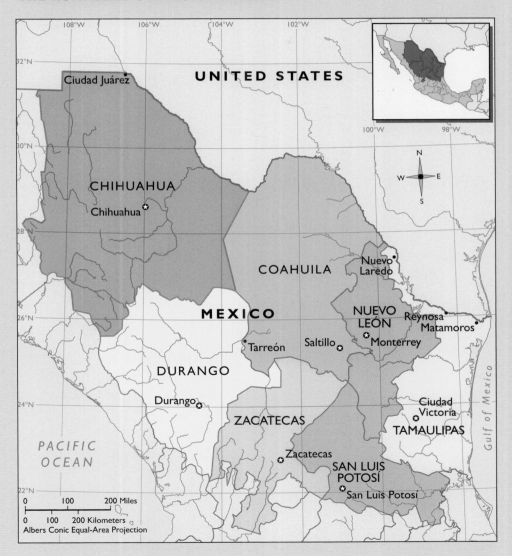

UNITED STATES

Ciudad Juárez

CHIHUAHUA

Chihuahua

COAHUILA

Nuevo Laredo

MEXICO

NUEVO LEÓN

Reynosa

Matamoros

Tarreón

Saltillo

Monterrey

DURANGO

Durango

Ciudad Victoria

ZACATECAS

TAMAULIPAS

PACIFIC OCEAN

Zacatecas

SAN LUIS POTOSÍ

San Luis Potosí

Gulf of Mexico

0   100   200 Miles

0   100   200 Kilometers
Albers Conic Equal-Area Projection

56

THE GULF STATES OF MEXICO

THE PACIFIC NORTH STATES OF MEXICO

Tijuana

Mexicali

UNITED STATES

32°N

BAJA
CALIFORNIA

Nogáles

Agua Prieta

Isla
Angela de
la Guarda

SONORA

30°N

Isla
Cedros

Hermosillo

BAJA

Isla
Tiburón

28°N

CALIFORNIA

Gulf of California

Ciudad Obregón

MEXICO

Rio Bravo del Norte

26°N

BAJA
CALIFORNIA
SUR

Isla
Carmen

Los Mochis

Isla Magdalena

Isla San José
Isla Espíritu Santo

Culiacán

Isla Santa
Margarita

Isla Cerralvo

La Paz

SINALOA

24°N

N

W   E

S

Mazatlán

Cabo San Lucas

PACIFIC OCEAN

22°N

0   100   200 Miles

0   100   200 Kilometers
Albers Conic Equal-Area Projection

NAYARIT

Islas
Marías

Tepic

116°W   114°W   112°W   110°W   108°W   106°W   104°W

57

58

THE PACIFIC SOUTH STATES OF MEXICO

SERIES GLOSSARY

adobe—a building material made of mud and straw.

Amerindian—a term for the indigenous peoples of North and South America before the arrival of Europeans in the late 15th century.

conquistador—any one of the Spanish leaders of the conquest of the Americas in the 1500s.

criollo—a resident of New Spain who was born in North America to parents of Spanish ancestry. In the social order of New Spain, criollos ranked above mestizos.

fiesta—a Mexican party or celebration.

haciendas—large Mexican ranches.

maquiladoras—factories created to attract foreign business to Mexico by allowing them to do business cheaply.

mariachi—a Mexican street band that performs a distinctive type of music utilizing guitars, violins, and trumpets.

Mesoamerica—the region of southern North America that was inhabited before the arrival of the Spaniards.

mestizo—a person of mixed Amerindian and European (typically Spanish) descent.

Nahuatl—the ancient language spoken by the Aztecs; still spoken by many modern Mexicans.

New Spain—name for the Spanish colony that included modern-day Mexico. This vast area of North America was conquered by Spain in the 1500s and ruled by the Spanish until 1821.

plaza—the central open square at the center of Spanish cities in Mexico.

pre-Columbian—referring to a time before the 1490s, when Christopher Columbus landed in the Americas.

FURTHER READING

Berdan, Frances F. *Aztec Archaeology and Ethnohistory*. London: Cambridge University Press, 2014.

Carew-Miller, Anna. *Famous People of Mexico*. Philadelphia: Mason Crest Publishers, 2015.

Coe, Michael D., and Rex Koontz. *Mexico: From the Olmecs to the Aztecs*. New York: Thames and Hudson, 2008.

Franz, Carl, et al. *The People's Guide to Mexico*. Berkeley, Calif.: Avalon Travel Publishing, 2006.

Grillo, Ioan. *El Narco: Inside Mexico's Criminal Insurgency*. New York: Bloomsbury Press, 2011.

Gritzner, Charles F. *Mexico*. New York: Chelsea House, 2012.

Hamnet, Brian R. *A Concise History of Mexico*. New York: Cambridge University Press, 2006.

Hunter, Amy N. *The History of Mexico*. Philadelphia: Mason Crest Publishers, 2015.

Kent, Deborah. *Mexico*. New York: Children's Press, 2012.

Levy, Daniel C., and Kathleen Bruhn. *Mexico: The Struggle for Democratic Development*. Berkeley: University of California Press, 2006.

Marley, David F. *Mexico at War: From the Struggle for Independence to the 21st-Century Drug Wars*. Santa Barbara, Calif.: ABC-CLIO, 2014.

Simon, Suzanne. *Sustaining the Borderlands in the Age of NAFTA: Development, Politics, and Participation on the US-Mexico Border*. Nashville: Vanderbilt University Press, 2014.

Williams, Colleen Madonna Flood. *The Geography of Mexico*. Philadelphia: Mason Crest, 2015.

INTERNET RESOURCES

Mesoweb
http://www.mesoweb.com/welcome.html#externalresources

National Geographic
http://kids.nationalgeographic.com/kids/places/find/mexico

CIA World Factbook
https://www.cia.gov/library/publications/the-world-factbook/geos/mx.html

History of Mexico
http://www.history.com/topics/mexico

INEGI (Geographic, Demographic, and Economic Information of Mexico)
http://www.inegi.gob.mx/diffusion/ingles/portadai.html

INDEX

PICTURE CREDITS

2:	Chepe Nicoli/Shutterstock
3:	Skyfish/Shutterstock
7:	Soft Light/Shutterstock
10:	Frontpage/Shutterstock
12:	Chameleons Eye/Shutterstock
13:	Frontpage/Shutterstock
14:	Jefferson Bernardes/Shutterstock
16:	Nataiki/Shutterstock
18:	Library of Congress
19:	Library of Congress
20:	UN Photo
21:	UN Photo
22:	Michele Pautasso/Shutterstock
25:	Corbis Images
26:	Bruce Raynor/Shutterstock
29:	Bruce Raynor/Shutterstock
32:	Corbis Images
34:	Corbis Images
36:	Corbis Images
37:	Corbis Images
39:	Corbis Images
40:	Jo Ann Snover/Shutterstock
41:	Moreno Novello/Shutterstock
42:	Victor Torres/Shutterstock
43:	Corbis Images
44:	Corbis Images
46:	Library of Congress
47:	Chao Kusollerschariya/Shutterstock
48:	Corbis Images
49:	Corbis Images
51:	Cristobal Garciaferro/Shutterstock
54–58	maps © OTTN Publishing

ABOUT THE AUTHOR

Ellyn Sanna has authored more than 50 books, including adult nonfiction, novels, young adult biographies, and gift books. She also works as a freelance editor and helps take care of three children, a cat, a rabbit, a one-eyed hamster, two hermit crabs, and a goldfish.